Richard James Allen's writing has appeared widely in journals, anthologies, and online, and he has been a popular reader at multiple performing arts venues, over many years. In 2019, a collection of poetry, *The short story of you and I*, was published by UWA Publishing, and a suite of poems, *Minimum Correct Dosage*, was commissioned by Red Room Poetry. Previous critically acclaimed books of poetry, fiction and performance texts include *Fixing the Broken Nightingale* (Flying Island Books), *The Kamikaze Mind* (Brandl & Schlesinger) and *Thursday's Fictions* (Five Islands Press), which was shortlisted for the Kenneth Slessor Prize for Poetry. *More Lies* is his first novel.

Well-known for his multi-award-winning career as a filmmaker and choreographer with The Physical TV Company, and critically acclaimed as a performer in a range of media and contexts, Richard has a track record for innovative adaptations and interactions of poetry and other media, including collaborations with artists in dance, film, theatre, music and a range of digital platforms.

Interactive Press
Brisbane

Richard James Allen is a poet, dancer, film director, actor,
screen producer, novelist, choreographer, yogi, archivist and
chess master – and only one of these isn't true.

MORE LIES

RICHARD JAMES ALLEN

Interactive Press
an imprint of IP (Interactive Publications Pty Ltd)
Treetop Studio • 9 Kuhler Court
Carindale, Queensland, Australia 4152
sales@ipoz.biz
http://ipoz.biz

© 2021, Richard James Allen, text; Alex Vaughan, photographs.
The moral rights of the creators have been asserted.

All rights reserved. Without limiting the rights under copyright reserved above, no part of this publication may be reproduced, stored in or introduced into a retrieval system, or transmitted, in any form or by any means (electronic, mechanical, photocopying, recording or otherwise), without the prior written permission of the copyright owners and the publisher of this book.

Printed in 12 pt Book Antiqua on 14 pt American Typewriter Semi-bold.

ISBN: 9781922332646 (PB); 9781922332653 (eBk)

A catalogue record for this
book is available from the
National Library of Australia

Other books by Richard James Allen

The Way Out At Last & Other Poems, Hale & Iremonger, 1986

To The Ocean & Scheherazade, Hale & Iremonger, 1989

Hope for a man named Jimmie & Grand Illusion Joe, Five Islands Press, 1993

What To Name Your Baby, Paper Bark Press, 1995

The Air Dolphin Brigade, Paper Bark Press and Shoestring Press
in association with Tasdance, 1995

New Life on the 2nd Floor (poems by Richard James Allen,
essays by Karen Pearlman), Tasdance, 1996

Performing The Unnameable: An Anthology of Australian Performance Texts
(edited with Karen Pearlman), Currency Press and RealTime, 1999

Thursday's Fictions, Five Islands Press, 1999

The Kamikaze Mind, Brandl & Schlesinger, 2006

Fixing the Broken Nightingale, Flying Island Books, 2014

The short story of you and I, UWA Publishing, 2019

for Money

Acknowledgements

The true story of the development of *More Lies* is a long and elusive one, but here are some moments where acknowledgements and thanks are due.

Early glimmers can be seen in a work of short fiction, "Story Story", which won the 1981 University Union Literary Prize at the University of Sydney, and a poem, "Un Poème en train de se faire", both published that year in *Honi Soit*. A first draft of the novel was written about a decade later, escaping the summer heat of an East Village, New York City apartment for Joan Pearlman's beach house writers' retreat in Woods Hole, Massachusetts. A decade on, an edited version was performed by the actor Christopher John Snow, as a 'shapeshifting monologue', at the 2000 Sydney Writers Festival, in a presentation directed and choreographed by the author. This text was shortlisted for the 2001 Griffin Award for New Australian Playwriting. And then, for reasons now forgotten, the manuscript went into the bottom drawer. A decade later, it came out again, when Karen Pearlman drafted adaptations for the stage and screen.

During the course of these explorations and evolutions, helpful feedback from the Literary Manager of the Sydney Theatre Company, Polly Rowe, as well as other colleagues and collaborators, led to further enrichment and refining of the underlying text.

Grateful thanks for feedback, encouragement and practical assistance over many years is due to: Lyn Tranter, Richard Roxburgh, Felicity Plunkett, Mike Jones, Matthew Campora, Ron Pretty, Rae Desmond Jones, Toby Fitch, Roberta Lowing, Samuel Lucas Allen, Annmaree J. Bell, Ulysses Oliver, Ben Ferris, Anton Enus, Nicholas Birns, Tara Moss, James Bradley, Jadzea Allen, Daniel Pardy, Martin Thorne and Jamie Hediger.

"The Road to Utopia" was first published in 2013 in *The Wonder Book of Poetry*, edited by Christopher (Kit) Kelen.

Heartfelt thanks to David Reiter for believing in *More Lies* and publishing it with such grace through Interactive Press. And warm appreciation to Alex Vaughan for allowing us to use her photographs.

Deepest thanks to my key editorial advisers, Karen Pearlman and Jocelyn Allen, for taking the coast road with this work.

Contents

Chapter 1: We Got Company, Ma

"Peters, Peters, Peters!" The voice was shrill and hard and had I known Peters I would not have recommended it to him. But Peters was nowhere to be found. Perhaps he preferred it that way, desired but unseen. Unfortunately, I am compelled to remember that Peters, dear soul...

Ah, but that was another story, in another time. Plenty of time for that. It is the woman calling out to him who intrigues me at present. Tall, willowy, immaculately dressed, well, I'll spare you the obvious metaphors though Lauren Becall comes to mind, why the divine creature has a delightful little golden handgun nestled behind my right ear, and is twittering sweet nothing encouragements for me, such as, "Keep writing, oh do keep writing, dear."

I would have hoped that making love to her earlier would have been enough, would have won her to my side, but immediately as we had finished, or shall I say, as soon as we were both quiet again and calm, she picked up the little trinket and positioned it in the closest proximity to my right eye, and, shall we say, bade me to continue, take up where I had left off, take up the pen again, young man, resume the keyboard.

Needless to say, I had to start the whole business again, as I had thrown the previous pages out the window at the moment when she had started to undress, as I conceived it would be far better to leave no reminders of the past once we had journeyed together through the doorway of love.

Excuse me! Hold on a minute! What the when, why and - let's face it - the hell am I talking about?

Well, what would you write about if you'd been made love to by a beautiful woman whom you had met less than an hour before and then been tied to a chair and told to write, while she held a magical little murder weapon to your head and screamed down the hallway to her accomplice, Peters, who had apparently been listening to and probably taping the whole proceedings from the apartment across the hall?

Well, be that as it may, I won't antagonize you too much, I do need at least one friend in this damn ghastly business. Perhaps Peters and the woman, the girl, the lady – her name, by the way, is Stricklandson – think I know something about something, which of course I do. Everybody knows something about something, but the trick is to know something about the right something.

And, by faith in such coincidental thinking, I fear I am tied up here writing my epitaph.

Chapter 2: Miraculously

What's this? Peters is on the phone. He is calling his mother collect. It appears that there was some plot to assassinate a visiting president, which has been temporarily foiled. Five bullets went astray and the poison turned out to be an obscure form of guava fruit. Miraculously, however, no one in the security forces seems to have found out that there was any threat and so they are going back tonight for another try. Their plan appears to be to use my apartment as a decoy base of operations. They feel that, with someone sitting, typing all day and night, no one will suspect them of hiding out here. It seems that they tried the same trick with Mrs O'Flattery next door, but she didn't know how to type so they left her in the fridge.

But what do the lovely Stricklandson and the hideous Peters, who has now entered the room, have to do with this story? And I myself, the great bystander, how did I come to be seated in the middle of this mess?

Perhaps they will enlighten me before pickling, I mean embalming, so at least I'll have a good story to tell in the afterworld? Without a good story, I hear, no one is going to give you directions or tell you what's going down up there. So that, by such bad luck, gentle reader, your faithful narrator would be left in no better situation than he finds himself in here.

Ah, yes, things are becoming clearer to me now. Peters and Stricklandson appear to be freelance operators working in the employ of a secret bureau of some foreign government. Their target, a rival tinpot dictator, is currently on a speaking tour of the United States. Tonight, he is addressing a special session of the United Nations on how he has solved the problem of illegal drugs in his country. Of course, nobody believes him, but it is all very proper and appropriate because whenever a visiting head of state comes to his country, he always pretends to believe everything he has to say also. In this way, everybody gets along very well, which is, after all, the whole point of diplomacy, is it not?

So, apparently, from what I can make out from this telephone conversation, in which Peters has spent most of the time being berated by his mother, who seems to be the head of this gang, the plan is for Peters and Stricklandson to place a small canister of poison gas amongst the flowers to be given to the president by members of his loving expatriate community as he greets them on the steps of the UN after his speech. The president will smell the flowers, the canister will explode, and poof, sweet revenge for whatever long-running soap opera of a grudge they think they have been carrying the water for.

They are planning to give the canister to a drug dealer who lives on the third floor of my building. He seems to have been a childhood friend of the president, but was kicked out of the country during one of the periodic official purges of drug dealers that allow the president to get so many billions of dollars of American aid. This guy, who is also a stand-up comic, tried out his material in some off-Broadway city for a while, then moved to the Big Apple and the Great White Way, where he couldn't catch a break and so took over his neighbourhood crack operation, running a steady flow of pimps, whores and Caucasian businessmen – white punters he likes to call them – up and down the stairs, in and out of, his apartment.

Chapter 3: The Trick,

as far as I can see, will be for me to slip out of the apartment sometime between the transfer of the canister and the payoff from Stricklandson and Peters to this drug lord comedian. Ah yes, I have an idea, and I'm reasonably sure I can afford to write it down as I think it out, since I don't think any of these guys is planning to read a word of what I write, which is hardly, I may say, flattering for a writer, but, in this case, perhaps just as well. I'll ask for a moment's pause, because, after all, no writer is never not going to get up and go to the bathroom, or walk around for a bit of a stretch and think what to write next. Then I'll suggest they move me into the small room and close the door, which, I will say, will mean my typing will create a greater reverberation in the inner courtyard of our building and will be heard more easily by any Federal agents snooping around outside. With the door safely closed behind me, because there is hardly enough space for one person standing, let alone seated, in this room, which is really a glorified closet, I will drag out my vintage synthesiser workstation, which I haven't used since I was tossing up between being a prog or glam rocker in the nineteen-seventies, quickly sample eight bars of the sound of a keyboard, and then set it to repeat to eternity, while I slip out the window, climb up the pipe onto the roof, and get away. This done, I can take a little stroll, get a papaya juice from around the corner, and catch the 11:30 rerun of *Guess Who's Coming to Dinner* (or it might be *The Thief Who Came to Dinner*) at Theater 80 St Marks. By the time I come out, history will have taken care of itself. I mean, let's face it, what the hell do I care about drug dealers, presidents, and the market segmentation of their illegal recreational supply chains? I've got enough problems of my own. Bye.

Chapter 4: The Strangest Muse

Well, folks, it didn't quite work out. They didn't go for the little room idea. I got the pee and the stretch, but apparently Stricklandson has still got her eye on me. Seems like she wants another round after the flower power has been delivered. My only hope now will be to put her to sleep with either the excitement or the boredom of the thing. Oh my God, there goes another plan; it appears that she wants to make love to me right here and now while I keep typing. This will definitely require some concentration. Wow, it appears I am quite stimulated, shall we say almost overstimulated, between the gun and Stricklandson's mouth and Peters watching. At least he's not masturbating. That would feel like this was some kind of a porn show. In fact, he looks rather disgusted and is turning away. More telephone calls. Well, that leaves me to bear the brunt, or shall we say the full weight of Stricklandson's intentions. I believe she finds this amusing, riding me crotch to crotch, hair to hair, follicle to follicle, with her little gun at my head to make me keep typing. I believe she's enjoying it a great deal. Please pardon any spelling mistakes. My God, Stricklandson has the most incredibly golden hair and the sharpest little teeth. This is the strangest muse I ever, ever, I ever...had.

Chapter 5: A Certain Fascination

Is this some kind of brainwashing torture to make me feel tenderly towards my captors? I can't help looking fondly along the lean body of Stricklandson as she puts on her bra and panties and zips up her dress. It's nice not to have the gun to my ear for an instant, though I'm fairly sure I'll be seeing it again. No, Stricklandson seems to have forgotten about it – she is talking to Peters, who has his hand over the telephone receiver. Perhaps, if I keep on typing, they'll forget to chastise me with the gun. Is this what socialisation is all about? Teach me to discipline myself? Well, yes, I am writing, but, in this case, I'll just be using it as a subterfuge until I can get the hell out of here. Maybe if I think good thoughts, like, "Alright, alright, when I get out, I will go to the police," then I'll be more lucky about it. I can go to the movies another night. That theatre's been closed for years now anyway.

And yet I'm starting to have a certain fascination with this Stricklandson woman. I mean, oh, you know what I mean, how did a beautiful woman like this ever get mixed up with a bunch of ugly mugs like Peters and this drug dealer who has a sad story but hasn't been given a name and is, therefore, I am sure you would concur, the most likely person thus far in this story to be expendable? As opposed to the rather magnificent Stricklandson, about whom any chivalrous gentleman would insist on knowing: What was the path that led her to it? At what point did it seem like a good idea? And when was there no turning back?

Okay, who am I kidding? I am hardly a gentleman, and don't tell me we don't all know we are on…

Chapter 6: The Road to Utopia

backstage
go backstage
draw the curtains
turn out the spotlights
take off your make-up
& turn back into a pumpkin
jump into a television
& ask the actors who they really are
unedit the movie
& show the world backwards
put the apples back on the tree
the fish back in the sea
the carrots back in the garden
the ice cream back in the cow
or at least the carton
unnail your house
& send the wood back to the forest
pour the honey back into the hive
the silver back into the mines
let out the bathwater
throw the food out of the fridge
the feathers out of your pillow
the fillings out of your teeth
the rotor out of your car
unbottle the wine
unroll your cigarette
unwind the clock
unlock the doors
& get undressed to go out
pick up Finnegans Wake

& put the words back in the dictionary
cut each entry out of the encyclopedia
each country from the map
& throw them to the four winds
mix up every name & number in the telephone book
so that nobody knows who's who
unthread your bedclothes
take the cartridge out of your printer
& print out unreadable invitations
asking the in-laws over for dinner
& if they come
& they always do
put on your pajamas
don't shave
rub the dandruff back into your hair
put the ice-tray into the oven
& roast the chicken in the freezer
fry your underpants
& put the pancakes in the washing machine
unmake the recipes
& serve the ingredients separately
unmix Coca-Cola into
a carnival of wine glasses
tell funny stories
about how you pegged up junior to dry
& sent his clothes off to school
or kicked grandma
& kissed the cat goodnight
then put the dirty dishes
straight back into the cupboard
& throw the whole party out
with last week's dishwater
beat your machine gun into a plough
bring back Martin Luther King
& Marilyn Monroe & Lenny Bruce

& if that's not possible
get back into the womb
& ask to be born in better times
or turn yourself inside out
& jump off the Empire State Building
screaming
I'M SUPERMAN

& FLY

Chapter 7: Aw, Where's Your Sense of Humour?

Better get used to it. I'll be dropping these things in every now and then, in fact whenever I can and feel like it, like songs or dance numbers in an MGM musical. How the hell else is a person supposed to get their old material out of the bottom drawer and published, if not by slipping it into any spare space that catches their eye, especially their own memoirs, for Chrissake! Why, I had something published in a CIA report once, but that's another story, except that I will say that, boy, they take everything so seriously over there, way too seriously to my way of thinking. Not that you can't believe everything you hear, except, really, do you believe everything you hear?

Hm, seems like (or is this just wishful thinking?), Stricklandson and Peters are arguing. Seems that whomever he was talking to on the telephone (could it be his mother again?) says that there's been a switch and the operation's off, at least for tonight. Seems like they have mislaid the whereabouts of the assassination payoff, which was a secret map to the hidden location of some Spanish gold. Seems like they have to get out of here as fast as possible, because the FBI is coming. The mother says destroy the evidence, which happens to be me, since Mrs O'Flattery across the way will probably be frozen solid by now, considering how badly these old fridges need defrosting. Now it appears, though I can't quite tell because Stricklandson and Peters are arguing violently in another language, that Peters wants to slit my throat and toss me out the window without delay, whereas Stricklandson wants me to stay alive awhile. Peters seems to be calling her a slut and she is beating him about the face with her gold lamé handbag.

Perhaps I could lift up my laptop and smash Peters over the head with it and then go off to the Bahamas with Stricklandson on one of the many credit cards that must be in her handbag.

I know, I'll leap out the window, catch a vine and swing to the next rooftop, and be away. Only when I get to the other side will I remember that New York is not that kind of jungle.

I'd better wake up – enough dreaming, something's happening. Stricklandson and Peters have made a decision. They are coming towards me. They are rushing towards me. Christ Almighty they are…

Chapter 8: Freeze-Frame

Perhaps in this, what appears to be the last few moments of my life, I can suspend time for an instant, or prolong the instant, by an act of memory, an act of flashback, a classic storytelling device, and what is storytelling but a voice against death, as IJselling, bless his dead heart, said about dear old Scheherazade, bless her dead rapture.

But how very rude of me. I haven't even introduced myself.

Let's see…am I a famous man, am I a wealthy man? Have I done great acts, have I altered the state of things? Am I kind, compassionate with others, am I at peace and in health with myself? And, since I am not an entirely selfish person, I cannot help but wonder who you are, dear reader, my only companion along this road of wonders, memories and – what are they called? Oh yes – old chestnuts.

Are you still listening?

What little nugget of golden truth or gossip do you want me to bury in the hills of these pages? What dirty little secret?

Ah, how adorable! My favourite! A temptatious mini-sidebar entertainment, a dainty delicacy detour…

Chapter 9: Down Memory Lane

Part the First: A New Language

Iwas born in Algeria, long before the war for independence. My parents were traders there, of a modest sort, though, when my father's import-export business failed him, he moved quite happily into a position with a larger firm and spent the rest of his days taking orders rather than giving them. My mother played the piano, another one of those stories of a woman who might have been a concert pianist, but she went away to the colonies to marry a trader.

By the time I was ready for primary school my family had moved, my father's firm deciding he might do better with the company's accounts in Cairo than he had in Algiers. I was forced to learn a new language, almost, as it were, overnight, as if I were expected to read a book continuously that was in English until page twelve and then began in Arabic halfway down page thirteen. This began for me a long series of assaults on languages and with these campaigns much travel as I felt compelled to relive over and again my childhood trauma.

I stopped at the thirteenth tongue, however; I was weary of my battles and, having carried them through, I seemed to have outgrown their fruits as I became too old to travel and too senile to remember, so that my vast encyclopedia of words began to sit more and more on the shelf, in the library, in its embossed jacket, terribly grand, a talking piece at cocktail parties, but moth-eaten and forgotten, the pages sticking together like cliché and truth, two lovers that refuse to part.

Part the Second: Family Music

I had two younger brothers and a sister, with whom I have long since ceased to correspond. The last I heard of the boys, the first to be born into our fourth-floor apartment is now selling collectible video tapes in Memphis, while the youngest is a star in a daytime soap, which I have never seen. My sister died some years ago in an unfortunate accident, which I would rather not discuss here, or anywhere for that matter, as I was rather fond of her.

But, when we were young, we were all together, playing like notes on a dissonant score, our melody lines occasionally forming mysterious atonal chords. My parents, the authors of this music, seemed alternately to delight and recoil from this discord, or, in their happier moments, to ignore it. Each of us played our instruments loudly or as best we could, none of us finding exactly the implement that suited our fingers and lips immediately. As we grew up, each down the line tended to inherit the music and instrument of the last, like a set of hand-me-down old clothes, until we finally threw it off or snuggled into it far more deeply. Do we still carry those violins and trumpets with us today, or are they hidden in the music of our playlists? On such musical staves the cacophony of our lives is written.

Chapter 10: Think Fast

Yes, like, but not like, think pink. We are back in the apartment. (Or are we? Well, you've got to believe me about something, haven't you?)

Peters and Stricklandson are still frozen in time like cardboard cutouts announcing the remake of a B-grade movie. If we were outside a cinema, I could just mosey on by and accidentally bump them over.

If we were outside a bookstore... Oh, that would never be... Those two uneducated sods – I bet they haven't read a good book in donkey's years. Hell, I bet they've forgotten how to read. Certainly, by this point in this text, I could say anything I wanted about them; there is no chance they could get this far, unless they started at the end and read backwards, and then only in the next hour or so, because after that I'll be pages away.

So, what tip of which iceberg shall I reveal before we slam our Titanic into it? Tell you what, I'll end this chapter by giving you a tiny glimpse. Peters and Stricklandson are my brother and sister.

Chapter 11: Which Part of This Do You Have a Problem With?

Now how can this be, I hear you saying, this joker is telling us he is a hack writer being held hostage in his New York apartment and forced to type as an aural decoy to distract from the argy-bargy criminal maneuverings of his sister, who is a femme fatale, and his brother, who is a gangster? Except that his sister is now also apparently dead and he has *no uno, sino dos* brothers, one who is in the soaps and another selling dirty videos or something. If this is fiction, it's stranger than truth.

Too right, sweethearts, I come from a family of entertainers, that is, after my father died, or rather, disappeared over the rainbow in search of his own personal old man and the sewer, liars, basically, let's not mince words, scoundrels, and I, while not the producer, that's Ma's job, am their scriptwriter. It's not like I do it willingly, or anything. I do find writing an extraordinarily daunting task, and so they have to tie me up and put a gun to my head, but most of the rest is a lot of cock and bull, my favorite specialties, though I am a strict vegetarian, and don't go in for any kind of meat eating or killing, myself. My sister, well, that's incest and there's no other word for it, and quite frankly I don't mind it at all in this particular case, though I certainly wouldn't want to let them know that.

But you want me to get on with the story.

Chapter 12: Story Story

Don't you know by now that there is no story? I mean I could narrate a chain of events punctuated here and there by flashbacks and flashforwards and flashes to the sides. But what would be the use of that? You can read that sort of thing in the newspaper.

Is there something you want me to say? Is there something you expect me to say?

He kissed her lips, her neck, her breasts. Her whole body pressed forward. It was delicate and soft, yet warm and hard. His hand ran lightly over the gentle curve of her belly and slid in under the folds of her dress.

Sex! Is that what you want? Or perhaps something else?

Pow! Violence.

How about Romance?

"Never mind," said the tall blonde commissioner of police to the frightened woman. He put his arm around her comfortingly. He was big and strong, and she felt safe and warm in his arms. He smiled reassuringly down at her.

"We'll see he doesn't bother you anymore," he said. "Here, use my handkerchief to dry away those tears." She looked up into his deep, kind eyes. Nobody had ever spoken to her like that before.

Will there be a happy ending? Not in the way you expect.

Chapter 13: Lights Out, Sweetheart

Here I am, halfway through, alright, alright already, hardly begun the promised land of the story of my life, and there are Stricklandson and Peters about to axe me, but frozen in the moment, now looking like some kind of a cheap ginormous cut-out picture postcard cartoon of David and Goliath outside a temple somewhere, but probably a bit harder to bump over given the number of men in black with semi-automatic weapons likely to be hanging around in the shadows like shadows since...

And what? Well, was I telling the truth about Peters and Stricklandson being my brother and sister, or was that just a tiny take-off of delirium? Let's just say I can't quite form the memory in my head. I remember some kind of growing up experience, but the faces aren't quite clear, sort of illegible, like a newspaper you think you're going to be able to read then you see it's in a foreign language. That said, my present is always a foreign country and nothing in my head ever smells familiar. Oh boy, sometimes I just love talking!

My God, what's that noise? Peters and Stricklandson are moving again, defrosting out of their frozen moment, rushing (well, maybe that's an exaggeration, let's try melting) towards me, Peters with – yes, I can see it now coming out of his shoulder holster – a gun in his hand, and Stricklandson – thawing ice maiden, glaciated jezebel, that she is – with a tear in her eye, and there's a, yes, that's what it's called, a terrific banging on the door. At my door.

It's Marly, it's my friend Marly. Well, hell, I don't actually like the old bastard, he lives across the hall and always wants to borrow my something or other or tell me that his section of the roof is leaking and why isn't mine, and have I been schtooping the landlady? Good old Marly, I've never been so happy to hear his soup pan tapping at my door.

And I know, even if Peters and Stricklandson don't, that he won't ever let up, he'll think I'm just trying to avoid him, which I usually am. I turn down the TV, dim the lights, turn off the water, if the bath is running, and lie low. But he always gets me. The wonderful bastard. And today he's going to get Peters and Stricklandson. Boy, they look scared. They don't know even as much as I do about turning down the lights and so on. Hell, they probably think he's FBI. Maybe he is FBI, undercover. My God, they've lost their heads, they're shooting at the door, Marly is screaming, the dogs in the apartment below me are barking like crazy. What am I doing still typing this story? They've shot the light bulb!

Chapter 14: Blackout

Don't ask me to believe
all that vampire,
werewolf, slime monster stuff!
Since when were
Bela Lugosi or Boris Karloff
experts in electrical de-circuiting?
They always work the late show,
they'd never make it to night school.
I bet some local punk
just kicked in our fuse box.
Whichever, it's too dark
to stumble about,
just to make sure my pot plants
haven't strangled the cat,
& my budgie hasn't turned into a crow,
& the steak & kidney hasn't reconstituted itself
as Frankenstein in the fridge.
The TV's starting to blink & sigh & gurgle
like a goddamn baby. Don't
dribble on my new carpet.
& don't start again
with that used car business
or I'll kick your face in.
I'm feeling so edgy tonight.
Maybe I'll go & wake up my buddy
uptown a couple of blocks
& chew it over with him.
&, that's right, his sister's
staying over for the weekend.
She'd look so cute in her pajamas,

half-asleep & standing in the hallway.
Course his old lady'd
probably bite my head off.
3 o'clock in the morning.
I'd better switch off this doggerel,
before one of us turns into Mr Hyde.

Chapter 15: Hard to Believe

It's hard to believe it, but Peters and Stricklandson are gone. They rushed out over poor Marly's dead body and leapt down the stairs, shooting the dogs that were scratching and howling at the door of the apartment below. I don't know how they did all that in the dark. I am still tied up and typing by the light of the battery of my laptop computer. It occurs to me that it's a good thing, in a way, that I've been typing all this time, because, when the police come, they'll know what happened and know not to blame Marly's murder on me. On the other hand, everybody in the building knows how I can't stand, that is, I never really got along with, the old codger. Maybe I shot Marly after a violent quarrel over a teapot and then I tied myself up. Maybe this cock and bull story proves it was premeditated, I couldn't have come up with it in the time between the murder and the time the police arrive. I must have been planning it for days, or at least hours. Who's going to believe a lot of hooey about bombshell blondes with golden guns speaking in foreign languages, evil villains deeply attached to their scheming mothers, and a failed assassination attempt on some dodgy visiting president, who is by now probably on a plane to who knows where? But they are going to find Mrs O'Flattery, frozen like a popsicle in the apartment next door, and I'm going to be the only one in the whole building, in the whole world, it will seem, who knows anything about it. God, I wish my mother and father had taught me the difference between right and wrong, the truth and lies. I mean, I mean, I am so glad my mother and father taught me the difference between right and wrong, the truth and lies. Well, whatever, I am certainly in a bind now, how the hell I ever got tied up with this problem, I'll never know.

Maybe if there hadn't been something, something, something about Stricklandson I couldn't put my finger on, I would have broken out of this mess, taken Peters on, and one of us would be lying out there in the street, eight floors down. And that damn fool Marly would have been bothering people still. Mrs O'Flattery, well, there was nothing I could have done about her, any more than anyone else in the building could have done anything about me. Wow, I can hear those sirens now. Somebody's called the police. Which does make me think, though. Maybe somebody else could have done something about me. Or maybe they still can. I mean every time there's a murder in one of those old movies, there's always someone who saw the victim just before they died, or the murderer after or before they left the scene of the crime. It's my only and last hope. What I've got going for me is human nosiness. And what I've got against me is the fact that everything is strange in New York.

Chapter 16: Human Nosiness

"Did you notice anything strange, anything out of the ordinary, Ma'am?" asks the officer. "There's not anything normal in this place, officer, you know that."

Oh my God, I can already see the flatfoot's interrogation, like a door-to-door product survey mashed up with a coming of O drama:

"Look, Mrs Robinson, you're not being very communicative.
They don't pay me unless I fill in all the blanks.
& anyway this isn't just a job,
I'm not a computer, you know,
I've got feelings of my own.
I'm not being rude.
What do you mean, I'm too personal?
Ok, ok, let's forget it, Mrs Robinson.
I'll try the people next door.
Anyway, I have to go & check my car.
The last time I left it in a place like this,
somebody threw a brick through the windscreen
& stole my heart. Never leave anything
you don't want to lose in the front seat of your car.

"You know, Mrs Robinson,
if you'd only answer my questions,
just this once, just this time,
we could really,
we could get this thing,
whatever this fling thing is,
started."

At which point, the police officer:

    a. 'unhousel'd, disappointed, unanel'd',
    b. tired and bamboozled,
    c. jilted and repudiated,
    d. all of the above,

will break into another kind of rap, an irrelevant, tangential spoken word poetry all his own (which I wish you could hear, but you will just have to imagine), as he sashays through my ajared door.

Chapter 17: This Falls Under the Sad but True Category

Sirens. And people screaming. Where am I?

Fear wakes you up. It makes you think clearly. At least for a time. Then it wears you out. It's the adrenaline rush. Suddenly I'm exhausted. I don't even know why I'm typing any more. I guess it has become a form of thinking. A way of thinking. A way of trudging forward with a sleepy mind. I am in a police station. I am in a cell. I am surprised they let me keep my laptop, but perhaps they figured I would be able to order my thoughts better that way. Perhaps they figured I might eventually communicate through it. You see I didn't say anything to them. I couldn't. I don't know why, I couldn't speak. They assigned me a lawyer. I don't think I've been charged with anything. Just held for questioning. I think they can do that for a certain amount of time before they have to either charge me or let me go. My lawyer said they want me to have a psychiatric examination. They don't know if I committed the murders or am just in a catatonic shock for having witnessed them. I hardly know myself. They have read what I have written so far and I don't think they quite know what to make of it. Most murderers apparently don't write fiction, so I guess that's on my side. At least they know about the possible existence of a Peters and Stricklandson, I think they have a search out on them. They've brought in the drug lord, but my narrative doesn't actually implicate him in the murders of Marly and Mrs O'Flattery, and he never got the canister. And, since they are probably already on the take for his drug trafficking, I don't know what they could charge him with, even if they wanted to, maybe conspiracy to commit murder, but that means unravelling the whole plot. And I'm pretty sure they think it's mainly just a knot tied up in my mind.

Chapter 18: Nothing Was As It Had Been

When I got home, nothing was as it had been. That is to say, where my lawyer dropped me off, from her gleaming white Mazda, was somewhere in Texas or Nevada or somewhere. She pointed to a little shack by the road and said, "There it is, your home sweet home, sweetheart, and you're frigging lucky to be there, if you ask me, bud. It's people like you that make me sick I ever got into the legal profession." And, with that, she was away, a spit in the wind. Don't let them fool you that all those female lawyers are cute. I mean, I'm talking about the inside. She might have had a cute butt – I mean pantsuit – but did she have a cute soul? Well, who knows, maybe she really did go to Radcliffe and really thought I had shot up Marly and iced Mrs O'Flattery and knifed Johnston and KO'ed Rodriguez and all those other raps they tried to pin on me. I mean they even thought I had been somehow responsible for – oh, we won't go into that... But my lawyer, Liefkowitz, she told them I wasn't a garbage truck, I wasn't a dumpster, I wasn't a catch-all for all those dirty unsolved cases that were cluttering up their records and statistics reports. No sir, they couldn't pin those murder medallions on this poor, wounded veteran who was just visiting from Nevada (she exaggerated a bit, but they were scared as hell and weren't about to check up on her facts, after all everybody knew that Liefkowitz was the daughter of a war hero and that she would never lie). That filthy writer who had owned the apartment, now he was scum, he was truly degenerate, they could pin the whole US army on his tail as far as she cared, but not this poor young visitor to the vast ugly city, who'd been caught up in the worst possible misfortune while he was supposed to be having a little fun, like any other boy his age. This kind of thing was bad enough when it happened to natives of New York, as it seemed to every night, but guests of the metropolis could not be manhandled without the whole five boroughs becoming a black eye on the face of the nation.

Chapter 19: Some Pretty Drastic Means

That's right, you guessed it. Liefkowitz saved my ass alright, but, by some pretty drastic means, she changed my identity. The cops were out looking for me in all the backstreets of the naked city, and I had landed in Nevada, dressed in the clothes of some kind of a cowboy. I don't know why she did it, Liefkowitz, I mean. Her dad was killed in the trenches or on D-Day or on the Korean Peninsula – or perhaps he was blown up in Saigon or Kuwait or Kabul or Baghdad? The fragments from one explosive ordinance blur into another. Maybe she always wanted to do a favour to a veteran with a Purple Heart. When she couldn't find one, she made one up. She fucked me, too, of course, but only in her imagination. I mean we did it, alright, and she was good. But who she was fucking was some shining knight way off in her mind. I was happy to help out, it felt kind of artistic, in a way, creative. But afterwards, she looked me in the eye with a strange kind of hatred and didn't say anything more until she threw me out of the hired car in the middle of nowhere.

Beautiful country, though, no doubt about it. And a beautiful woman, no doubt about that, either. Maybe I'll meet her again one day under more propitious circumstances. Maybe we could settle down somewhere and raise some army brats. Pay the country back. When they grow up, they could become defectors, smuggle themselves over to whomever is the enemy at that point and give away the national recipes. That way, as soon as that country became our country's best buddy, which wouldn't take too long, easily within their lifetimes, they could return to the US under an official pardon, join the National Security Council and advise the leader of the free world when they decide on granting our former enemy most favoured nation trade status. Immediately afterwards, they could leave government to become special consultants to several Middle Eastern financed banking companies making a killing on the opening up of new high tech armaments markets.

Be in the right place at the right time. That's what my grandfather used to tell me. Or, if not, make it the right place at the right time.

I miss my grandfather! But there is no use waiting around for him, anymore than the other fellow.

Chapter 20: The Rubbish of My Mind

I don't know what happened to Grandfather and all his other apposite clauses, but heaven help me this book I am writing – this new work I am writing oh oh oh oh oh don't tell me – it writes itself, it drives like Julius Caesar, or Gaius would have, if only he'd had a Pink Cadillac with crushed velvet seats, then he could have tiptoed through the tulips over Hadrian's Wall and made it all the way up to the top of Scotland to meet the lost twelfth tribe of Israel, before U-turning down to the backdoor of the future Buckingham Palace to catch up, in camera, with the illegitimate descendant of a one day long-to-be-forgotten English king, all the while ignoring what might be discovered on the other side of the family tree about the organization of suffering through time travel into the illumination waiting room, including a Spanish-looking boy a lot darker than his siblings; it feels many-minded, it fights for a home life, it loves me, it hates me, it worships the ground I walk on, it wants to ruin my career, such as it is, out here in the middle of a dust bowl desert with only a gas station and a Coca-Cola machine for company; it knows that if it mentions any word beginning with 'c', including copyright, it will get an immediate FBI file, that is to say if it doesn't have one already in which case it will be upgraded to a higher level of security risk; it thinks it may be a cheap (like life) but nonetheless true (like life) series of lies, and in the meantime it promises (it lies) to prove that all language is a series of clichés people can bear to hear just one more time around.

Whatever the truth is (date is), the truth is I am becoming someone else. Hell, I can't even remember who I was way back whenever it was I was who I was.

Chapter 21: The Homeless

My words are homeless.
This text is homeless.
If I had a home, I'd give it one.
If I had a home, I'd give this text a name.
If I had a home, I'd give my home a name.
If I had a home, I'd give myself a name.
If I had a home, my name might be
Anything but
Everyone who reads this
When I write it will be dead,
Everyone who doesn't read this
When I write it will be dead,
Everyone who didn't read this
If I didn't write it will be dead.
Shall I compare thee, honey?
To be or not to
One two three o'clock
Four o'clock rock.
God isn't dead,
He's just camping out
In an expensive condo somewhere,
Under an assumed name,
Along with Elvis
& a select group of
The other disapppeareds.
The homeless are our heroes!
Homelessness is the next great,
The only great, American frontier.
The homeless are on the welfare of the imagination.
The homeless have a special place in my imagination.

But do they have a special place in my home?
God asked me this question
(God likes to ask the questions),
& you can bet He's homeless too.
I'll Admit It, This Poem
Isn't Much Good For The Homeless,
Said The Sincere & Well-Meaning Author,
As He Turned To Go Home.
All He Could Do Was Keep Turning, Turning, Turning,
Until He Became A Star In The Sky.
& That, Sweet Child,
Is How The Stars (& Stripes) Were Born.

Chapter 22: Bad Command or File Name

Fuck, I have to thank you, Liefkowitz, you raving whore, you sweltering lunatic, you prize-fighting legal superbitch, no, I mean it, I really want to thank you for sending me out into the Siberia of the American frontier and thereby wiping my slate clean. New name, same face to be sure, but hell I don't look so bad, in fact I'm kind of cute, but be that as it may – new memory! Thank you, Lord, Liefkowitz, the Goddess, Chance, who or whatever. I wasn't sure I could face another day as myself. I needed the relief of becoming someone else. I got it. But who am I now?

> *My name is...*
> *My name is...*
> *My name is...*

My God, I must have a name. I must have had a mother, a birthplace, a baptism, I must have had a name. Somebody must have seen me off. I look myself up in my computer. "No matches found." I try again. "Bad command or file name."

Even this book is a wanderer, carried around on a computer chip through time and space; sure, not outer space, but this observable human space; this land, sea, air, fire and imaginary space we imagine we inhabit, we dream on. Ah yes, the theoreticians (especially the old school new school ones) will be sure to agree that this book is writing itself

> *and who am I,*
> *without name or face,*
> *without food,*
> *without sleep,*
> *without desire,*

to disentangle them from their intricate affairs, their liquid entanglements with words, with the delicacies of books?

A me,
within me,
I cannot describe,
neither male nor female,
child nor adult,
dead nor alive,
a me,
before me,
and after me,
yet within me.

I wanted to call this book *Safe*, so it might keep me that way, but I will probably call it *More Lies*, because I am an honest man.

(I guess you can test the outcome of that theory and practice flip-flop, trial out this potential KPI balloon, by thumbing to the dust jacket of whichever cheap edition of this book you have picked up in a second-hand store. Not to say that you are cheap, but really, as much as who am I, really, who are you, really, and, as much as your choices define or illustrate who you are, really, then how much of your per capita income do you invest in anything of cultural value, really?)

Chapter 23: ¿Cuánto?

Somebody has offered me money for this book. They have come up to me and flashed their fucking greenbacks in my face. Why does everybody think money will get them anywhere, everywhere, including into my book? Fuck that shit. What do they think money is – a little piece of heaven? Well, tell me if I'm wrong (yes, I mean it, motherfucker, send me a postcard care of my publisher, which is currently General Delivery, Nevada), I don't want no pennies from heaven.

How much?

I told the guy who wanted me to turn my book into a talk show, who offered me money if I'd change it, just a little, mind you, nothing spectacular, just the usual sex, drugs, sex and rock 'n' roll, not that he'd read what I've written or anything, just that he assumed there was something wrong with it, I told him to fuck off, but I agreed he could pay me back for my wasted time by taking me to his favourite local whorehouse. I went into the waiting room, got shown the house selection, and picked a blonde, making sure that the guy put his cash on the table before I went into my room. Boy, the blonde was something. To tell you the truth, I never frequent whorehouses, as far as I can remember, but somehow I found it difficult to say no to this agent or whatever he was. He was so apologetic about having bothered me, suddenly he seemed to have a genuine interest in my well-being. He started running down this list of directors and stars that wanted to buy the film rights. But I was more interested in the blonde. And the blonde, oh boy! Don't believe that stuff about blondes not being passionate. Though I don't know why she kept asking me to type the whole time we were making love. And I don't know what was a nice girl like that doing in a dingy place like this? I mean, we are talking about a down-home place of business here. The guy, who told me earlier his name was Peters, told me later that she was the illegitimate daughter of some northern European count or something. She had a strange name, pretty, but a little dangerous, like poison ivy: Strick something. Anyway, I'm looking forward to seeing her again. She could be a real pal. Oh yes, I remember, that was it: Stricklandson.

Chapter 24: Home Is Where the Art Is

Whoever the hell I was in my past life, or at least in the life I have left in the backroom of memory, I probably wasn't a good judge of character. It pains me to say it, as I assume myself to be a good Christian soul, kind and compassionate to the stranger, welcoming and understanding of the other, but, Jesus, that Peters fellow is a creep, that's clear to me now, and, as for Stricklandson, there is something sweet, but very peculiar, about her. I don't know what the hell they want from me, but they keep asking me questions, as if there is something hidden in my memory that they want to recover. And they keep wanting to touch my book. You'd think I knew the whole intricate history of the stealing and the hiding away of some shiny loot, to which secluded spot my book was a map. I threw them, though, I promised I'd rack my brains for some memory of what they were looking for, all the while feigning a naïve ignorance of what they were actually talking about. Then I told Peters I needed some money so I could check into a real hotel for a hot bath and a good night's sleep and maybe even a bit of a massage. And I wouldn't let him or even the beautiful Stricklandson print out my manuscript or borrow my laptop overnight – "just for a little peek at the masterpiece", they said. Wow, maybe they should read it! Hell, I should have a read of it myself. Maybe there's something here even I don't know about.

With the cash I hopped a four-seater charter plane. I can't tell you where I'm going, I'm afraid. Nothing personal, kind reader, but I really don't know who to trust these days. I mean, how did Peters and Stricklandson, if they were following me, know where the hell I was? Obviously, my lawyer, Liefkowitz, tipped them off. Or maybe you did, dear reader? Sure, I agree with you, though I am quite aware you are trying to distract me, what stake did Liefkowitz have in my survival? I mean, I was as surprised as you were that she helped me out at all, considering she despised me so much. On the other hand, she did help me. But you, dear reader, into whose care I have entrusted my most secret thoughts and activities? I never questioned you, I carried you with me, so to speak, I assumed you were on, as well as by, my side. You got to know everything, such as there was to know. You got to see everything of my doubts and hopes and fears. Or at least that's what you thought. What you didn't know was that I may have been onto you from the very first. How do you know this whole thing hasn't been an elaborate façade to throw you off the track of what was really going on?

What was going on? What is going on? One thing I can tell you, since you don't know where I'm going, is that I know where the gold is. That's right, the Spanish gold, the blood money. How do I know where it is? Because I have the map, of course.

Chapter 25: Laugh at Will

Yep, you guessed it. Or maybe you didn't. Mother, the head of our favorite gang, got here first. Here where the conquistadors hid their loot. But the beautiful thing is, it isn't here, and she doesn't know where it is. Of course, I don't know either, but I'm not going to let her know that. I mean, obviously I need some kind of bargaining chip or my life isn't worth a fried clam. Perhaps I did something with it during one of my forgetful spells, I tell her, during one of my little turns – it's so convenient to call them that, isn't it? I promise, on pain of being turned into fine purée by a couple of her henchmen, my country cousins, Mohawk and St Somethingorother, to try to shake the new location of the gold down like a banana from the tree of my memory. Of course, the real problem is that I have no idea where the stuff is stashed, not consciously, at any rate. The only person I can think of who might know, or give me a clue, having heard me murmuring in the night, is Liefkowitz, my lawyer.

I call for an appointment with Ms Liefkowitz under my assumed name, the one she gave me to hide my degenerate identity as a New York writer. Mother waits with Mohawk and St Somehoworother outside the head office of Liefkowitz's law firm in Chicago. I take the elevator up more flights than there should be numbers. I have to come out with a detailed map of where the Spanish gold has been moved to or I'm chopped liver. Liefkowitz receives me in her corner office, the one with the hawk's nest vantage point that guarantees that she would be one of the first people to see advancing armies coming from two directions. It wouldn't be polite or professional to meet a client with the impeccable credentials she has bestowed upon me anywhere else. You have to admire that kind of consistency in a person, who will do the right and proper thing, even if it destroys them. I don't blow the cover, not just yet at any rate, I appear in one of those smart suits with dyed-blonde hair and blue-tinted contact lenses. Hell, if you blink, you'd probably take me for Stricklandson. Maybe, in a strange way, Liefkowitz does. Of course, she would.

Chapter 26: What?

Oh! Didn't I tell you Liefkowitz was a lesbian? And that means... What? Oh! Didn't I tell you I'm a woman? That's right, Liefkowitz changed my sex when she changed my identity. You do want the truth, don't you? I know you had me pegged as a dick all this time. Well, dyke or dick, as you will recall, Liefkowitz and I didn't exactly leave things cordially. But sometimes one has to revisit the past and this is one of them. You see, the truth is, Liefkowitz and I have known each other since we were kids. We had our first sexual experiences together, under the covers of Mother's bed. Later on, we drifted apart. And when she was assigned my lawyer completely out of the blue on that night in Manhattan, well, it was a strange reunion. We took up the old affair, and she got me the hell off the rap, for old times' sake. But then she dumped me in the desert. She is an out-of-sight-is-out-of-mind-er and she thought that she could drop a bomb in the desert without it affecting the rest of the world. But here I am, come back to haunt her, probably expose her and ruin her career, because I am pretty clumsy about those sorts of things.

Chapter 27: Sort of Blink

Liefkowitz knows where the gold is alright. That is why she made such a big thing about changing my identity and dumping me in the desert, instead of defending who I am (or was) and leaving me alone in my garret. So much for old times. Well, maybe that's not fair, things get pretty mixed up sometimes. She is happy and pissed as hell to see me, but I don't leave the office until she's spilled the beans.

Sure, I wanted the gold. In a strange way I am a Robin Hood of sorts, if you sort of blink. I can imagine a lot of good things to do with that money, a lot of good causes to give it away to.

But, at this point, back in the twin-engine plane, with Mother and Mohawk and St Somewhereovertherainbow breathing down my neck, and Peters and Stricklandson to follow, that money is never going to set up an arts scholarship for downtown experimental writers, choreographers, filmmakers and performance artists. No self-help shelters for homeless people. No AIDS or gender reassignment funding programs. There's my island, here's my chance, come with me, little laptop. Big smile, grab the parachute, go for the door – and bye, bye, Mumsie!

Chapter 28: Are You Still Here?

Sliding up the sky, floating down the sky, this rushing silence.

Here, life couples with death.

Letting the darkness catch up. Slowing down for the light.

Peace doesn't know the difference.

Except...

Except…

You! Are you still here? Jesus, like a bloody conscience, *you* I am having the most trouble getting rid of.

You keep eavesdropping on my thoughts and there is very little I can do about it, except hand out disinformation, which, luckily, I am very good at.

OK, crunching down on terra firma, since you are obviously here for a reason, let's begin at the beginning. I am a firm believer in platitudes. Yep, you bet I am. On worn out tracks many people have travelled. Truth in repetition, in pattern, in rhythm. *Dance, dance, dance.* Are you still here? Did we begin yet?

Oh, what do you want, you didn't really expect I'd change my mind and lead those bloodhounds to the pot of gold, did you? Why would I do that? Did you think I'd lead you, or even my publisher, assuming I get one, to the end of the rainbow? Perhaps you thought I'd fall asleep and mumble out the road map in my dreams? Not a chance. The only person I'd pass on that kind of information to would be a character in a fairytale. One that couldn't get out of his or her colourful little book world. Not too many of those left any more, I'm afraid. Like they always told you, if you don't believe the magic, how can you expect it to come true?

You want to get into my dreams? You want the driving map of my dreams? You want to find the combination to the big safe? Let me give you another perspective on that idea. Try to get *out* of my dreams.

Who says who is asleep and sleepwalking here? Who says who is surveying whom? Who's to say I haven't been monitoring you ever since you picked up this God damn book? Now you didn't think of that, did you? Eavesdropping in on you, watching your every move this whole time, through some tiny apparatus implanted in this book? Yeah, a microchip receiver, a video camera. Who's to say this whole text hasn't been a trick to keep you in the one place, or, more precisely, to allow you freedom of movement, but for us to know exactly where you are at all times? And exactly what you are doing. Yes, yes, an elaborate homing mechanism, a tracking and location device. Quite simple in its construction, actually, but clever in its tactics. Read your opponent before he or she or they can read you, or, as we see in this case, while she or he or they think they or she or he are reading you. Make him or her or them think they or he or she have you on the run.

Chapter 29: Ulterior Motives

When I began this story, I did have some ulterior motives, I have to admit it. But, to tell you the truth – though why should you believe me? – all I can say at present is that I want you to know that I have your very best interests at heart. If I didn't, I could never do what I am about to do. I mean, I was brought up like you probably were, to get what you want but not destroy anybody else in the process. Unless they were a traitor to your country. And I don't think we need to cast you in that light, do we? I mean, if I set the FBI or MI5 or ASIO or Shin Bet or FBS or whatever is your country-specific equivalent organization to look into it, to take a poke around, to turn over a few random cojones, we both know they would find nothing untoward in your record, would they? A couple of little indiscretions here and there, but hell, nobody gets by without a few of those, not even a saint. No, I fully believe that you are entirely clean and clear and uncontaminated in all your dealings; and I don't intend looking into any matters you or your family and friends and colleagues may find embarrassing. If, of course, there are any matters you would like to get off your chest at this time, feel free to go over those with me now and thereby save a great deal of pain and anguish at a later date. Please jot down any salient points on matters of this sort in the space provided below. In this way, we can be sure that no one has overheard your statement, which, of course, we'd like you to sign, just for the record, and which, rest assured, will immediately and securely be scanned into our zero-knowledge cloud storage. We want you to know that, as outlined in our Privacy Policy, everything you write will be kept strictly confidential and will not be used against you. In fact, by confessing fully and freely now, you will be providing yourself with a kind of immunity from prosecution at a later date. Now, don't forget to sign (or, if you can't remember how to hold a pen, or your hand cramps up, not to worry, you can just murmur, mumble and whisper what you have to say and we'll pick it up, it's all part of our friendly service):

Confession

I,_____(name),

of_____(address),

being of sound mind and body, do freely confess to:

_____

_____

_____   _____

_____

_____

_____

_____

_____   _____

_____   _____

_____

_____

_____

_____

_____

_____.

*Signed:*_____

Thank you. I knew I could count on your cooperation. Now, don't forget, everything you have written will remain strictly between ourselves. And, while I can't say, having had a glance through, that I'm not a little surprised by a few of the items you've brought up, it's not my job to judge, and, in any case, I can't say I don't like surprises. A couple of mini-jolts every now and then keep the old ticker going, and, you know, I wouldn't want to fall asleep on the job, especially since it's surveillance. How would that look?

Chapter 30: Wakey-Wakey

So, where was I? Where was I when? Back then or the other time or the first time? Jesus, did I just nod off? Well, I don't know if you are aware of it, but it's quite difficult keeping talking and typing and tap-dancing on the ceiling and trying not to blink for this long. Not impressed? Alright then, forget it! Wherever the hell I was, or you were for that matter, forget it. Let's go on from here. And you can stop worrying about the monitoring business, and even the goddamn confession. I'll tell them I buggered up the tape somehow, you know, some technological crap, I left it too close to some dog-shaped magnet or toaster oven or something. And a giraffe ate your confession. Yeah, look, hell, I'm getting out of this job anytime soon now, anyway. Who wants to leave wiping their feet on the doormat? And, to tell you the truth, I've grown to like you. Yeah, I've grown genuinely fond of you, which happens to me every once and a while. I kind of get to like someone. They make me think that life's worthwhile. So, don't fuck up now, you hear? I got my hopes pinned on you and I don't want the little motherfuckers disappointed. At least not right away, anyway. I'll give you some leeway to make the God damn mistakes everybody makes in a little while. Till then, let's pretend you have already made them and you're already older and wiser but at the same time young at heart.

Now I'm going to tell you the truth…

Chapter 31: ...If I Can Remember It

It's like a dream,

already slipping away.

Dreams are like finger writing

on a mirror in a steamed-up bathroom.

However profound their subject matter,

they have no depth. They evaporate off the surface.

Look, I wasn't lying when I said that I never did mean to antagonize you too much, that I always did need at least one friend in this damn ghastly business. I still do.

But the truth is not my specialty. Don't look at me that way. It's just that it doesn't satisfy me. And I don't think it will satisfy you, either.

The truth is never enough. Or it's unlikeable. I know I don't like it. Who could ever like the truth, all those sordid details? My throat hurts and my tongue is all swollen up because I have told so many truths.

I am sick. I am very sick. I am sick inside. I am so sick that I am not sure I am even really all here. It feels like a part of me is missing. A very big part. I have a hole inside me that feels primordial like a dying star, that feels fathomless like a black hole, that feels illimitable like a vortex, which is imploding and then expanding out forever.

The truth is I am the nebulous memory of a supernova with the potential to be a whole new universe. But only when you watch me. Only when you listen to me. Only when you interpret my signs.

You are my quantum astrophysicist. You observe my future. You create my future. You are my future.

Don't look at me that way! No, don't turn away, either. Look at me, but just not with those eyes.

Don't you understand? I thought you, of all people, would understand. It doesn't really matter what I am saying, so long as I have your attention. The truth is I need you to hear me, to see me.

For all of this long and winding road you have allowed me to exist. Otherwise, I would have been only potential. Without your gaze, I am nothing.

Or is that what you want? Is that what you are waiting for now? To watch me evanesce? Like a ghost, like a memory. Something that only exists when it is brought to mind and then fades into the nothing with the fickle turning of thoughts. Are you that cruel?

Chapter 32: The Dark Rememberer

Once upon a time I told you there was no story. That wasn't true. There's always a story.

But you've stopped listening. Not that I blame you. You can't rest until you have tracked down the truth.

You remind me of something in the old world, where cold has a shape, a wave through time and space. An animal on the hunt, exacting a principle of nature, carrying life by the throat.

You want this more than I do.

I am the story. Don't ask me if I am true.

Chapter 33: Without Your Gaze,

I am nothing. The simplest of nothings. Hints of what might be, what might have been, perhaps even what was.

A flash of headlights across a broken windowpane. A breeze lifting a curtain. A hinge squeaking. A heavy thud. And then another. A muffled cry and then all quiet, except a dusky-eyed baby crying out as a black hole starts to appear in the centre of its universe. Boots on gravel, an ignition. A vehicle pulling away, turning into the night on a road to who knows where. A deed done, without explanation, that can't be undone.

Yes, in case you never quite believed that we had landed before, we are back on Earth now. Feet well and truly in the mud. Back in time. Buried in statistics. Fusty old files. A long-forgotten crime scene. One of many, but this one particular to this child, its inheritance. Left with a handful of wordless seeds. When it grew up, it planted the dead bodies of all of its family in the pages of this book and look what grew.

Are they coming back to you now? All those old wives' tales? All those oddly truncated, always-changing-gears, family stories told to you sideways, like sliding a loose clutch through endless neutral in a rusty pickup truck? Stories thrown away like tossing bait into the river to attract fish. In their own secretly proud way, did your own uncles and aunts and all the good ol' boys of your town want you to find out, to investigate, to remember?

And so now? Who knows who is lost and who is found in the backwards and forwards of time?

This voice that was spared from death must now surrender to it. Whatever remains of our truths, lies, stories, and secrets will never be known, or, if glimpsed at once, will now be lost forever.

This voice was only ever meant to exist for a short while, I see that now. I hope its visitations were of a less violent sort than those which gave it breath.

One day you may wake up with the thought...

P.S.: Epilogue, Dénouement, This is the End, etc.

Oh, for Christ's sake! I told you, didn't I? Well, did I or didn't I? Didn't I tell you something off the record, off the book, out of the earshot of the microphones? Didn't I level with you because I said I liked you? Didn't I make some kind of special exception in your case? Didn't I give you a chance? Didn't I give you a break? What in the space shuttle fuck do you orbiting mean you don't crash-landing remember? Soon there won't be anything left, because everybody is throwing everything away. Am I right?

So, you forgot the fuck about it. Well, that's really too bad. And I don't just mean for you or for me, I mean for everybody. Because, as I told you, and this was the last thing that I remember, I wasn't going to remember anything anymore of what I had to say after I told it to you. Frankly, I do remember it had been an enormous effort to keep it in my head as long as I did. It was like something you keep kicking around a bathtub as the water runs out. Eventually, it's got to go down the drain. And it did. And it's gone, just like I told you it would be. I was only the guardian of that knowledge for so long, and then I had to pass it on. And I passed it on to you. And you say you've forgotten it before writing it down or putting it in a safety deposit box or telling it to someone else like I told you to do. So, everybody else, everybody who cares – if anybody cares, that is – will have to make up their own beginning, middle and end. Which maybe they always had to do anyway. Because that's what happened to the truth of this tale.

P.P.S. But don't take it too hard. You never know. Maybe it'll come back. Come back around like Halley's Comet. The best lies often do.

And then perhaps you will finally feel *safe*.

www.ingramcontent.com/pod-product-compliance
Lightning Source LLC
Chambersburg PA
CBHW030347030726
47499CB00003B/940